A First Guide to Learning French

A CHILDREN'S LEARN FRENCH BOOKS

BABY PROFESSOR

EDUCATION KIDS

Alphabets et Numéros Français

(French Alphabet and Numbers)

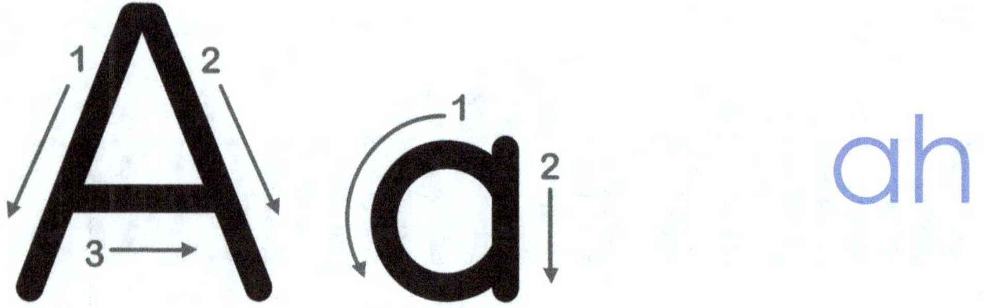

Airplane - Avion

B b

bay

B B B

b b b

Butterfly - Papillon

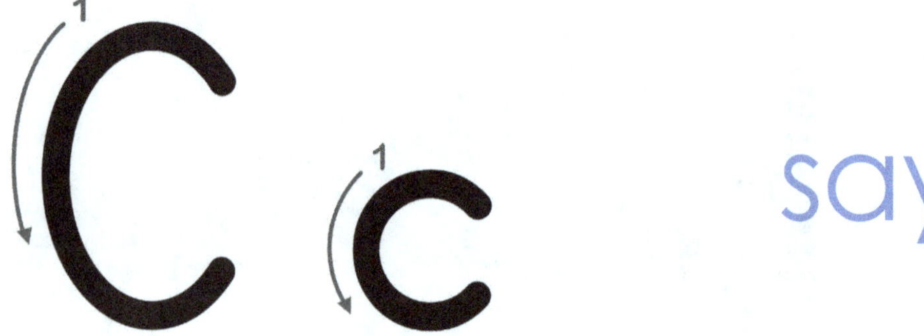

C c say

Cake - Gâteau

D d

day

Doughnut - Donut

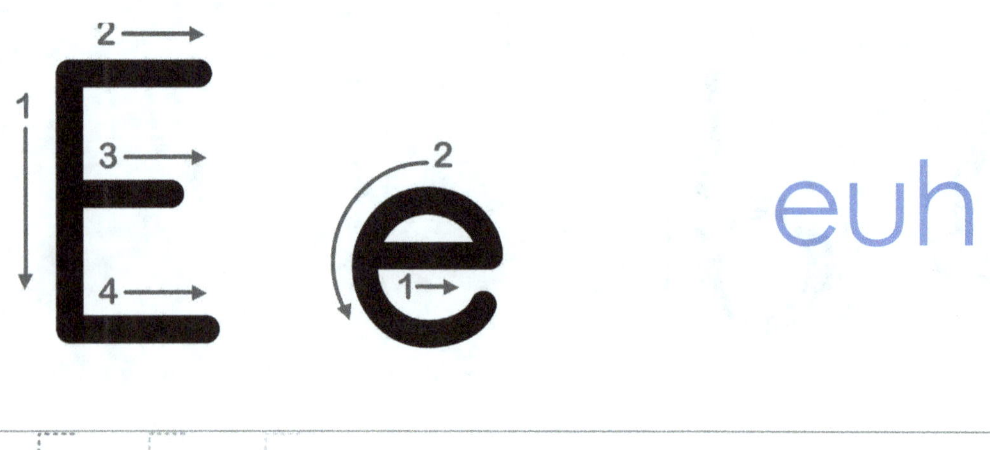

euh

Eagle - Aigle

Fish - Poisson

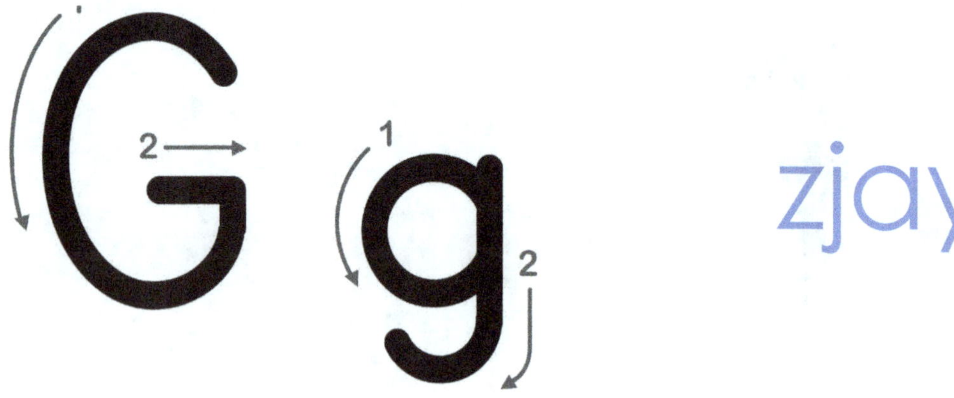

Grapes - les raisins

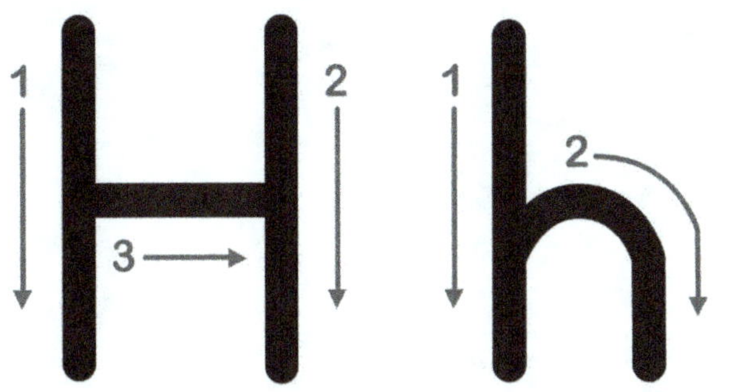

ahsh

House - Maison

ee

Ice cream - Crème glacée

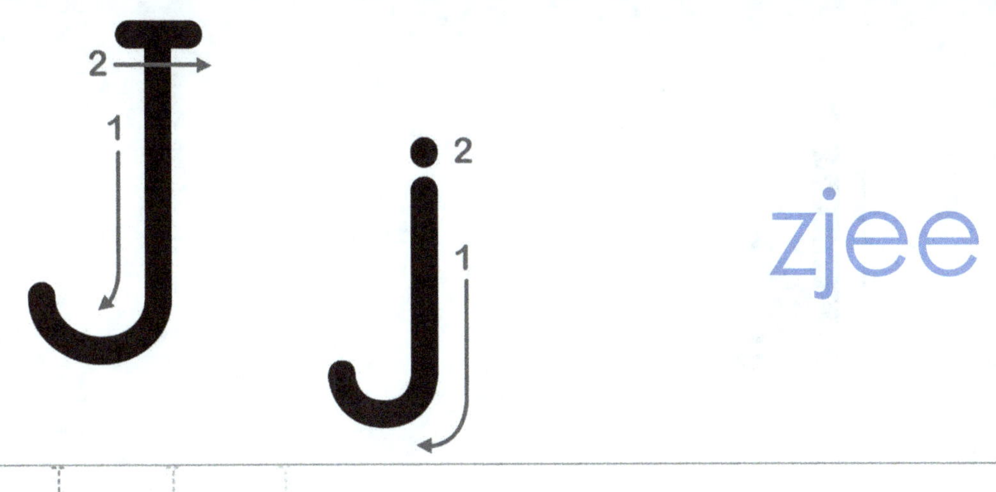

Jam - Confiture

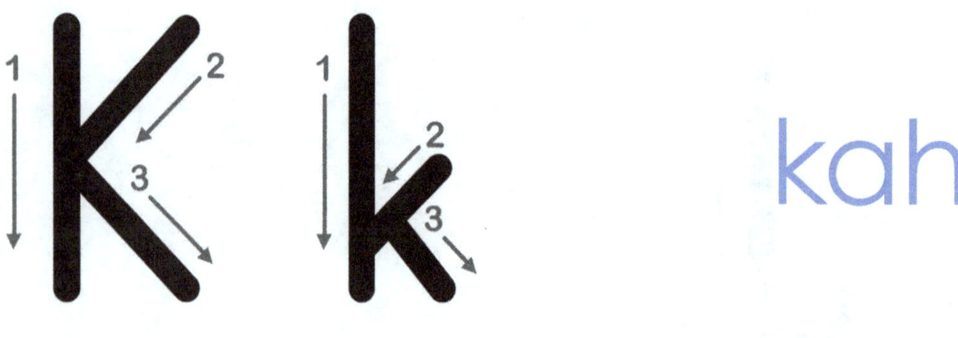

kah

Key - Clé

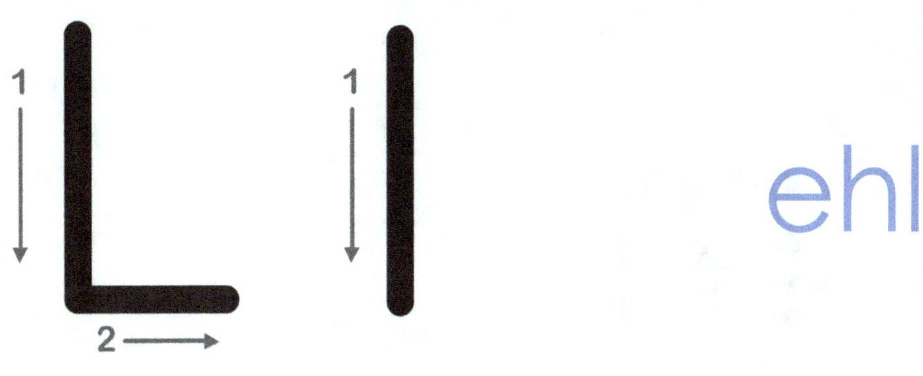

L l

Ladybug - Coccinelle

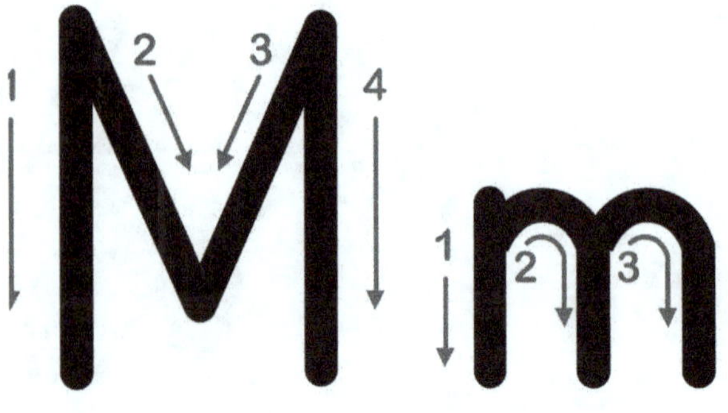

ehm

Monkey - Singe

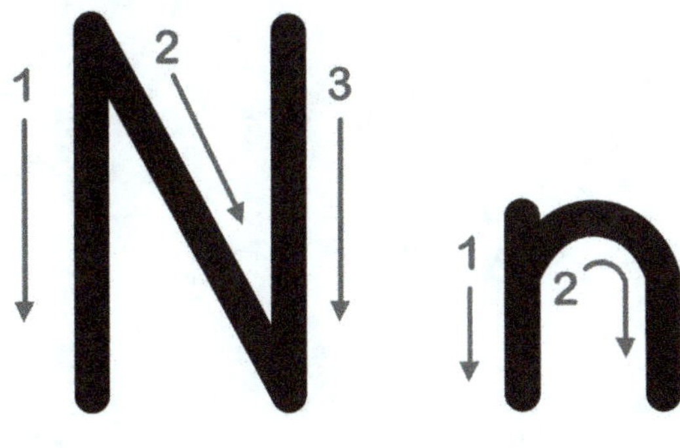

ehn

Nest - Nid

O o

oh

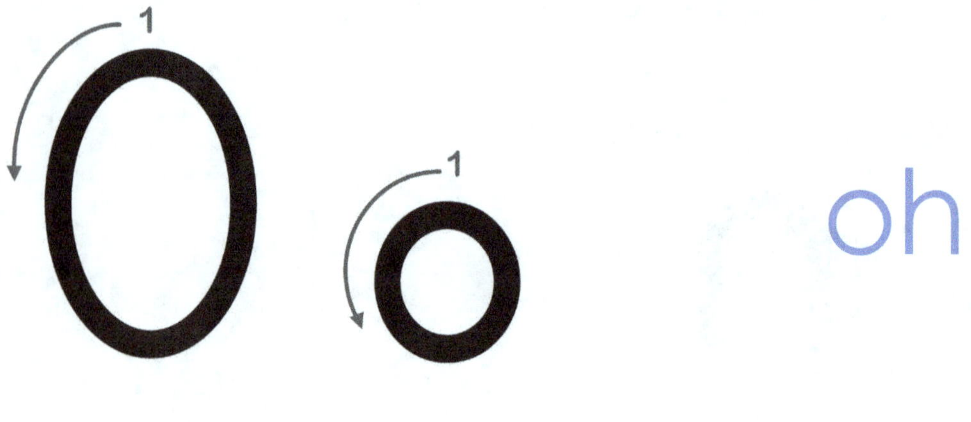

Owl - Chouette

Penguin - Manchot

koo

Queen - Reine

air

Rainbow - arc en ciel

S s

ess

Sun - Soleil

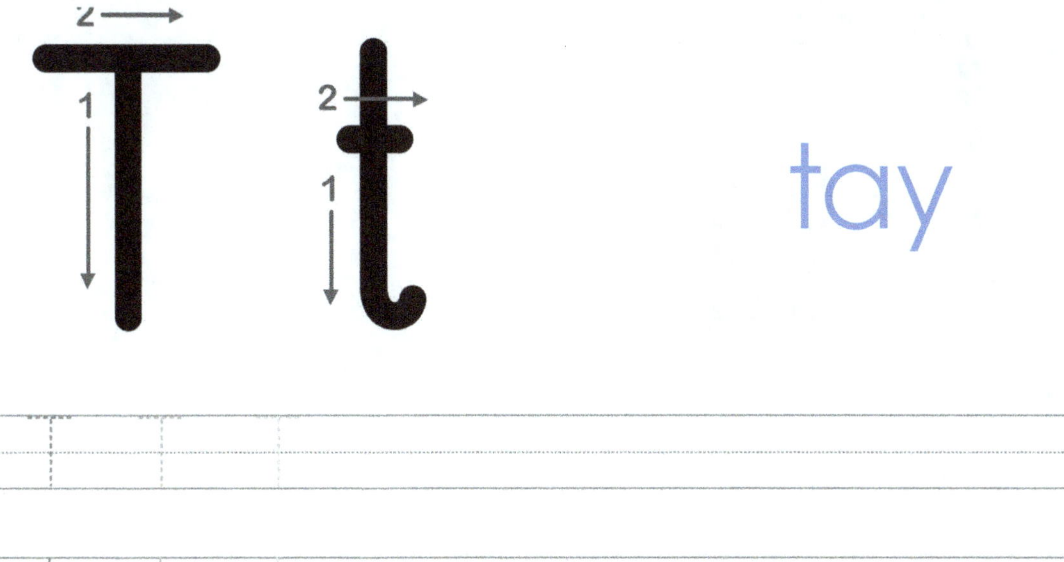

tay

Tree - Arbre

Umbrella - Parapluie

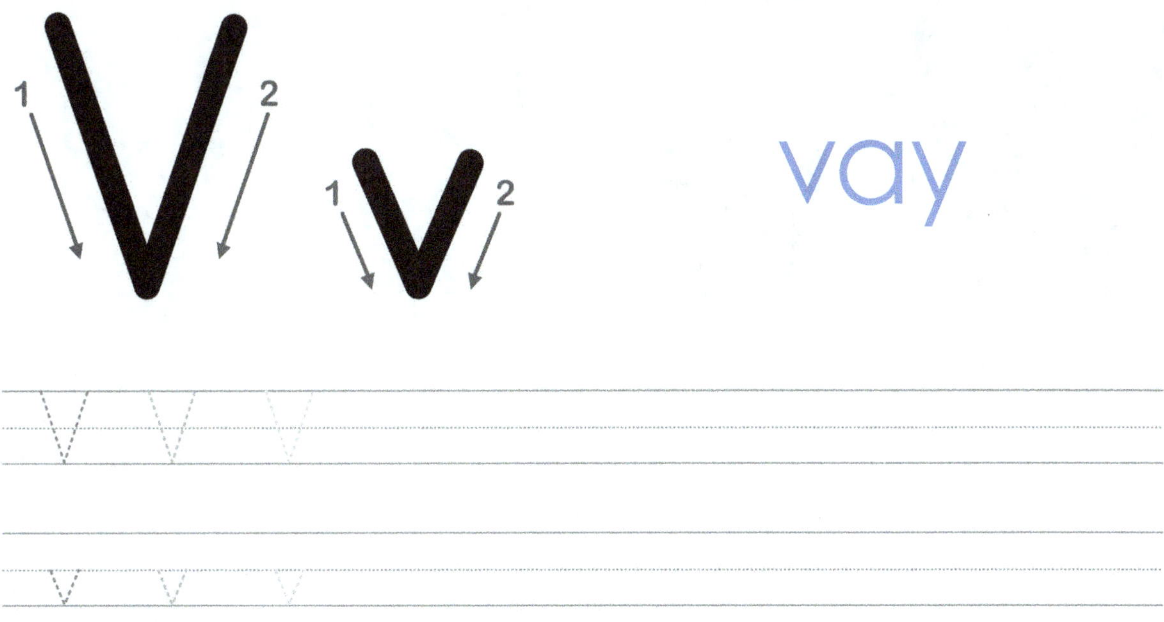

Vegetable - Légume

Watermelon - pastèque

zehd

Xylophone - Xylophone

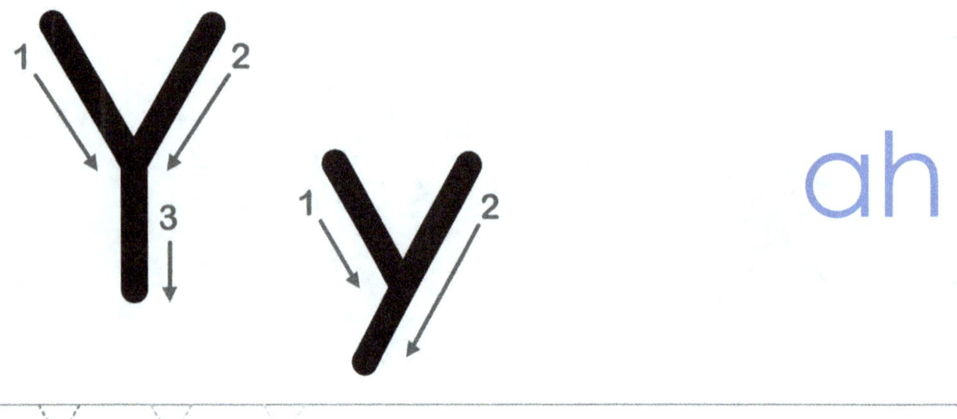

ah

Yogurt - Yaourt

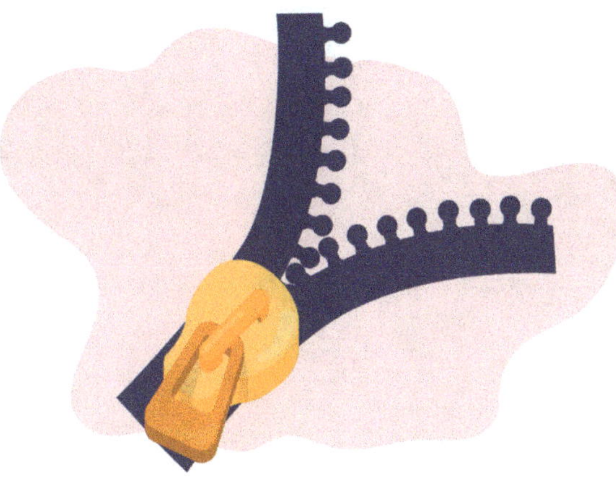

Zipper - Fermeture éclair

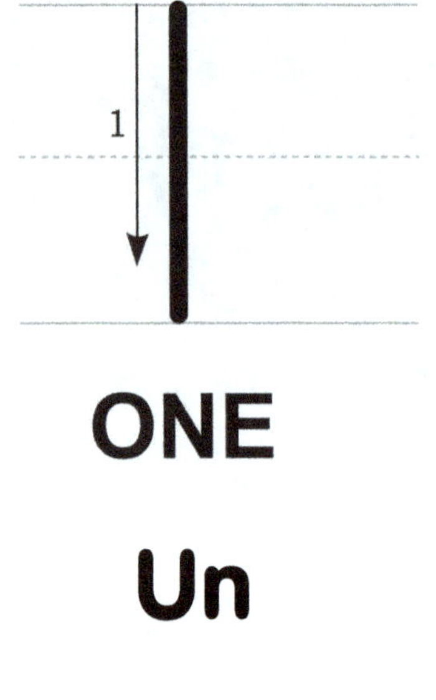

ONE

Un

2

TWO

Deux

3

THREE

Trois

4

FOUR

quatre

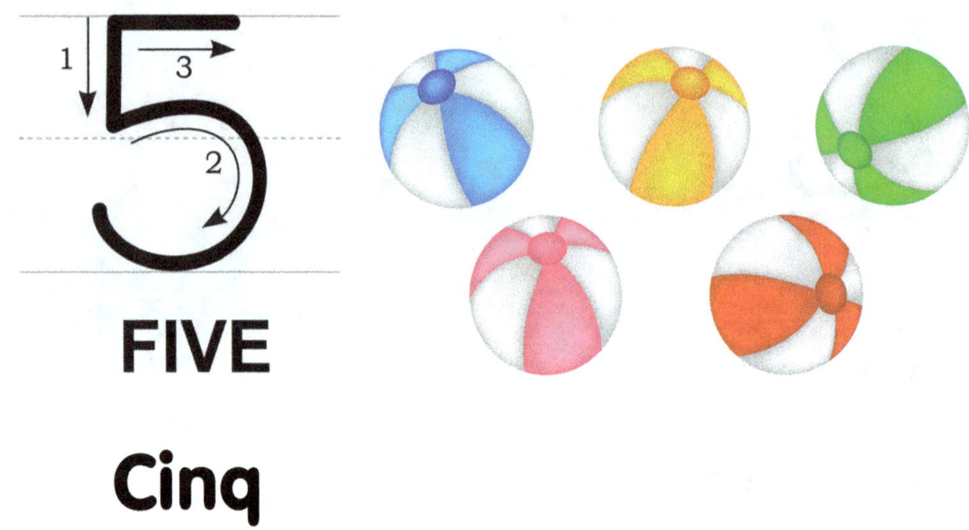

FIVE

Cinq

6

SIX

Six

7

SEVEN

Sept

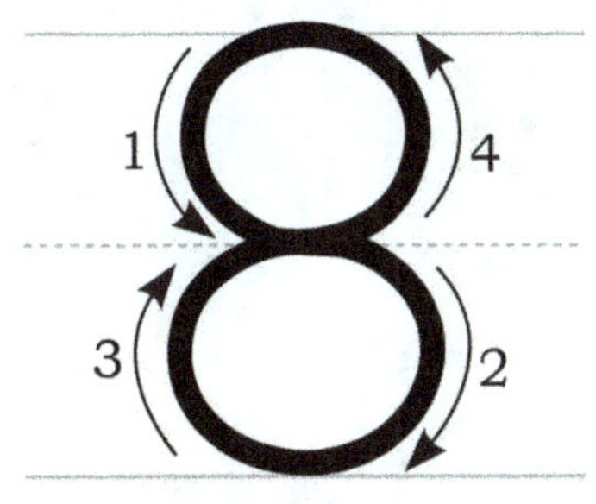

EIGHT

huit

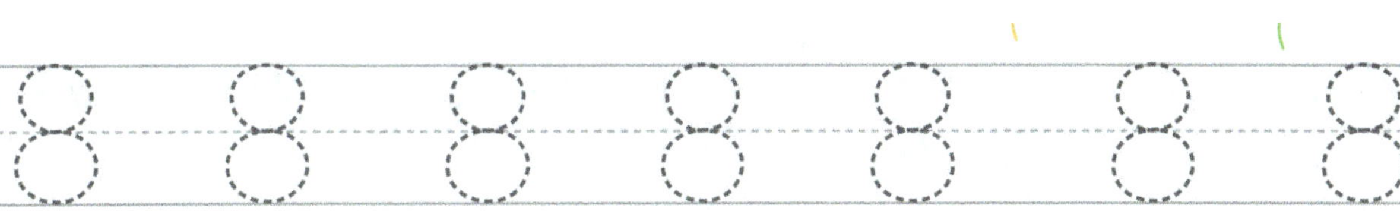

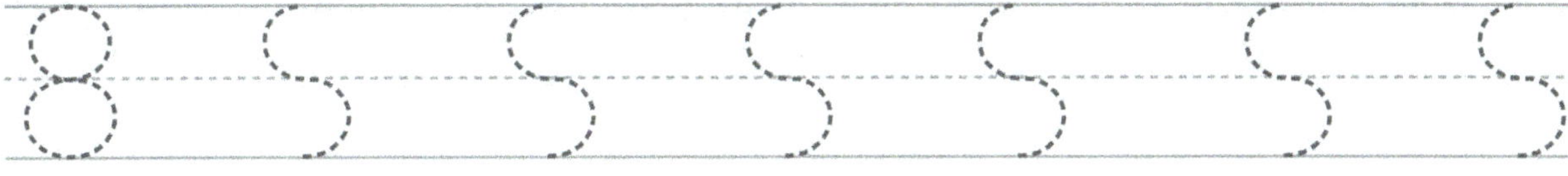

NINE

neuf

10

TEN

Dix

Visit

BABY PROFESSOR
EDUCATION KIDS

www.BabyProfessorBooks.com

to download Free Baby Professor eBooks
and view our catalog of new and exciting
Children's Books

www.ingramcontent.com/pod-product-compliance
Lightning Source LLC
Chambersburg PA
CBHW081149180726
48003CB00026B/2989